ROMANS 1:12

MENTORING
An Example to Follow

Gary Wilde, ed.

ChariotVICTOR
PUBLISHING
A DIVISION OF COOK COMMUNICATIONS

Victor Books is an imprint of ChariotVictor Publishing,
a division of Cook Communications, Colorado Springs, Colorado 80918
Cook Communications, Paris, Ontario
Kingsway Communications, Eastbourne, England

Scripture quotations are from the *Holy Bible, New International Version*®.
Copyright © 1973, 1978, 1984 by International Bible Society. Used by permission of Zondervan Publishing House. All rights reserved. Other refer-
ences are from *The Living Bible* (TLB), © 1971, Tyndale House Publishers,
Wheaton, IL 60189. Used by permission.

Editors: Barbara Williams & Greg Clouse
Designer: Andrea Boven
Cover Illustration: Mark Stearney
Cartoons: Rob Portlock

Recommended Dewey Decimal Classification: 248.832
Suggested Subject Heading: PERSONAL RELIGION, MEN

ISBN: 1-56476-617-9

1 2 3 4 5 6 7 8 9 10 Printing/Year 02 01 00 99 98 97

TABLE OF CONTENTS

Sorry, Johnnie, you can't have my mentor.

INTRODUCTION

WELCOME TO...

An exciting men's study experience! Whether you'll be meeting with others in a group, or just going through this book on your own, you've made an excellent decision by choosing *Encouragers for Men*.

The volumes in this series are for men from every background and denomination, men who typically meet with each other to share their joys and hardships, their life concerns and prayer needs, their spiritual insights and questions—in short, to share their lives. Groups usually meet at lunch break or during an early morning breakfast. Or they may meet in a home during the evening.

According to a popular men's movement, our society views men as: mostly self-reliant, unable to feel or express emotion, unconcerned about fellowship, using people but loving things, primarily competitive, and too macho. You are taking an important step toward changing that situation.

WHY THIS TOPIC?

Many men long for a group in which they can safely reveal their problems and receive the support they need to overcome them. Finding and befriending a fellow struggler brings tremendous encouragement, as men discover that they are not alone. The book you've chosen, *Mentoring: An Example to Follow,* emphasizes the importance of this kind of accountability, which is based on serious self-exploration and candid sharing.

What happens when men do not find a group where this kind of sharing takes place? They may bog down in their spiritual journeys in one of two ways. First, some men try to control their circumstances. This stance characterizes the man who says, "I believe I should be joyful; I should feel fulfilled. But I never seem to reach it. I try and try, but something always goes wrong." When faced with dissatisfaction in life, he tries to force the circumstances to change so that he can once again feel happy. It doesn't work.

Second, some men keep trying to "act the part." This is almost the opposite approach. These are the guys who try to act as though things are really working out great all the time. Not content to savor the blessings and joys God sprinkles into their years, they may pretend unbroken daily bliss. In effect, they begin to fake the Christian life, wearing the mask of continual victory. And of course that doesn't work for long either.

The third and more truly Christian approach to life is left to those who are learning to embrace the pain—the pain and the struggle of spiritual pilgrimage. It's not the easy route to take, but it is the most honest. It brings us down to a basic reality, that everything we are and have is a product of the pure, unconditional grace of our Heavenly Father. And here's the key point: This approach to Christian living cannot be done in a vacuum. It requires fellowship, mutual encouragement, and ongoing accountability as men meet together to discuss their progress (successes and failures) along with their need for prayer. That is the way they help each other live for God, all along the way to Christian maturity.

How to Use This Guide

For Individual Use

Any man can benefit from personal study of the stories, Bible passages, quotes, and questions in this book. Just set aside a few minutes each day to be alone and in silence with your Lord. Ask Him to show you what you need to be learning about fellowship in His church. When you come to statements that refer to a group, creatively adapt them to your own relationship with God or with people you know. Then try to put some of your insights into practical action.

For Use in a Men's Group

These sessions work great in a group of three to ten men. Make sure every man has a book and use rotating leadership each week. Participants should try to come to the session having read the chapter. But for those who come unprepared, the chapters are short enough to skim or read aloud during the group time itself. The key to the study format is simply "laying material out on the table" for discussion. Men will pick up on this and feel free to let the discussion move into their particular areas of concern.

Preparing to Lead a Group Session

See the *Can You Relate?* section of each session for your basic outline as you take your turn leading discussion in the group. When it's your turn to lead, your job is to act as a discussion facilitator, not a teacher. Before the session you'll spend some time thinking about how the readings relate to your own journey of spiritual growth. Answer the three questions below, and you will have all the material you need for generating discussion—because people will feel free to contribute their own insights, comments, and questions in response. (You will also find specific questions about your particular topic in the section *For Further Thought or Discussion*.)

► What experience in my own life confirms (or disputes) the material I've read?
► What themes or statements stand out to me as most important, significant, or controversial?
► What questions, comments, insights, or personal applications flow from this material?

Getting a Handle on the Format

Here are some explanations of the items you'll find in each *Encouragers* session. Items 2, 3, and 4 below provide the overall theme for discussion. Group members will choose the parts of these story-sections that strike them as significant, and they'll relate those stories to their own experience. The goal is personal application, in the context of group accountability, for the purpose of solid spiritual growth.

► *1. Check-in / Update.* Sessions typically open with each group member "reporting in." Sharing consists of "I" statements about life as it is at the moment: A feeling to report, a problem to share, a personal or spiritual growth question or insight, a summary of the week, a progress report/accountability check.

► *2. One Man's Story.* This opening vignette offers one man's experience with the topic. It is a personal, "how-I-see-this issue" report, intended to put the subject into the context of everyday life.

► *3. God Enters the Story.* These are printed Scripture passages related to the topic—there for your reference. Some groups will focus heavily here, others will simply let the Scripture serve as a theological boundary for the discussion. The fact is that "our story" (the way we actually live) often clashes with God's story (the call to deeper commitment and holiness). This creates a tension that makes for excellent discussion: How can God's story become, to a greater degree, the story of our own Christian growth?

► *4. The Story in Quotes.* These brief excerpts add spice to your discussion. They are sometimes profound insights, sometimes controversial thought-starters. Some group members will agree with the statements, others may disagree. The quotes are often drawn from the devotional classics, but can come from any source, secular or religious.

► *5. Can You Relate?* You'll find a set of four general questions in each session. The leader uses these questions to make up the basic "plan" of the session time. Sometimes your group will go no further than responding to these questions.

► *6. For Further Thought or Discussion.* Here you will find creative ways to explore the issues raised in this particular chapter.

► *7. Prayer Moments.* Each week, your group members will choose, how to use their prayer time. Varying the approach gives each group member a chance to pray in a way that is most comfortable.

► *8. Suggestions for the Week Ahead.* Here you're given practical life-response suggestions related to the week's topic. You may wish to use these suggestions to set up an ongoing accountability report to be given during each session. This is a way of inviting each other to check up on your progress. Each group member can choose suggestions that will help him take the first steps toward change.

► *9. The "Back Pages" Resources.* Be sure to check out the *Group Strengtheners* provided in the back pages of this book. You'll find: *Creative Session Starters*, a *Fellowship Day Idea Starter*, a *Video Night Discussion Outline*, and a *Weekly Prayer Record*.

So, ready to begin? Call the men, set a time and a place for your weekly meetings, and get started!

Call Them Out!

CHECK-IN / UPDATE

What's happening with you?
- A feeling to report
- A problem or struggle to share
- A personal or spiritual growth question/insight
- A summary of your week: issues/concerns/joys
- A progress report/accountability check

ONE MAN'S STORY

Early in the fall of 1964, at the adventurous, indestructible age of twenty . . . I set out for the "Dark Continent," asking not what my country could do for me, but how I could share the boons of Western civilization with other, apparently less fortunate people.

After several months of teaching young African men about congruent triangles, however, I was startled—and appropriately humbled—by a simple question while chatting with a student about American families.

"How is it in America that a boy is called by the men?" he asked, matter-of-factly.

I hesitated, wondering if perhaps my student were using improper syntax. "What do you mean?"

"In your own village in America," he replied, "how did the men come for you, when you were reaching the proper age to come out from your mother's house?"

"Oh," I said readily, smiling graciously, "in America, unlike here in your village, the mother and father both live in the same house, so that sort of thing really isn't necessary."

Clearly puzzled by my response, the young man moved as if to speak, hesitated, and then sat quietly, knitting his brow. Unsure what more to say, I changed the subject. . . .

I had occasion later to ask a Nigerian teacher to describe for me his own initiation rite as a boy. . . . [In his village] a boy lives with his mother until he reaches the proper age, usually about eleven. Then one evening the village elders and the boy's father appear outside the mother's hut, together with a drummer and a man wearing a large mask over his head. The word for "mask" is the same as that for "spirit," so as the masked man steps out first from among the men, both to call the boy out and to usher him from the mother to the men, the spiritual dimension of manhood is understood from the outset as primary and essential.

At the signal of a sharp drumbeat, the mask/spirit approaches that mother's door, dancing and shouting, "Come out! Come out!" After several retreats and then thrusting forth to announce his presence and intention, the mask/spirit rushes the mother's door and beats upon it loudly, *Bam! Bam! Bam!* "Come out! Son of our people, *Come out!*"

Eventually—perhaps after two or three such "approaches" by the mask/spirit—the mother opens the door tentatively, shielding her son behind her. At this, the elders and the father join in the chant: "Come out, son of our people, come out!" Significantly, the mask/spirit does not enter the mother's hut to seize the boy, but rather, waits for him to step out on his own from behind his mother. Louder the elders chant, sharper the drum beats sound, more feverishly the mask/spirit dances, and more firmly the mother protests—until finally, she steps aside.

It is the moment of truth for every boy in the village.

—Gordon Dalbey[1]

GOD ENTERS THE STORY

Then Rebekah said to Isaac, "I'm disgusted with living because of these Hittite women. If Jacob takes a wife from among the women of this land, from Hittite women like these, my life will not be worth living."

—*Genesis 27:46*

[Hannah] said to her husband, "After the boy is weaned, I will take him and present him before the Lord, and he will live there always."

"Do what seems best to you," Elkanah her husband told her. "Stay here until you have weaned him; only may the Lord make good His word." So the woman stayed at home and nursed her son until she had weaned him.

After he was weaned, she took the boy with her, young as he was, along with a three-year-old bull, an ephah of flour and a skin of wine, and brought him to the house of the Lord at Shiloh. When they had slaughtered the bull, they brought the boy to Eli, and she said to him, "As surely as you live, my lord, I am the woman who stood here beside you praying to the Lord. I prayed for this child, and the Lord has granted me what I asked of Him. So now I give him to the Lord. For his whole life he will be given over to the Lord.". . . So Eli told Samuel, "Go and lie down, and if He calls you, say, 'Speak, Lord, for Your servant is listening.'" So Samuel went and lay down in his place.

The Lord came and stood there, calling as at the other times,

"Samuel! Samuel!"

Then Samuel said, "Speak, for Your servant is listening."

And the Lord said to Samuel: "See, I am about to do something in Israel that will make the ears of everyone who hears of it tingle.". . . Samuel lay down until morning and then opened the doors of the house of the Lord. He was afraid to tell Eli the vision, but Eli called him and said, "Samuel, my son."

Samuel answered, "Here I am."

—*1 Samuel 1:22-28; 3:9-11, 15-16*

THE STORY IN QUOTES

If you went up to your mother and said, "I want the key so I can let the wildman out," she'd say, "Oh, no, you just get a job," or, "Come over here and give Mommy a kiss." There are very few mothers in the world who would release that key from under the pillow, because they are intuitively aware of what would happen next—namely, they would lose their nice boys. The possessiveness that some mothers exercise on sons!

—*Robert Bly* [2]

The central difficulty in becoming a man nowadays is that a boy sees so little of his father or other men. A man's work is now separated from his home. There are no men around for boys to model themselves after. Boys are almost exclusively brought up by their mothers and taught by women teachers.

—*S.I. Hayakawa* [3]

What does my own culture offer as a validation of manhood? The driver's license at sixteen; and freedom at eighteen to join the Army, attend pornographic movies, and to buy cigarettes and beer. The message is clear: becoming a man means operating a powerful machine, killing other men, masturbating, destroying your lungs, and getting drunk.

We are lost males, all of us: cast adrift from the community of men, cut off from our masculine heritage—abandoned to machines, organizations, fantasies, drugs.
—*Gordon Dalbey*[4]

It is said that life begins when the fetus can exist apart from its mother. By this definition, many people in Hollywood are legally dead.
—*Jay Leno*[5]

CAN YOU RELATE?

► Which one of the three story-sections above "rang a bell" with you? How?

► What personal story or experience comes to mind, in relation to these themes: (a) **the challenge of mentoring boys into men in our society;** or (b) **rites of passage—or "calling out"— for boys today?**

► What other **insights** came to the surface for you? What **questions** were raised in your mind? Do you have any **personal applications** to consider?

FOR FURTHER THOUGHT OR DISCUSSION

► Share about your relationship with your mother—both as a youth and as an adult (whether your mother is still living or not). What is the significance of the fact that the men of the Nigerian village wait for the boy to "step out on his own from behind his mother"?

► How would you characterize Hannah, as a mother to Samuel? Would you say that Hannah displayed courage? If so, what similar form of courage is required by mothers with their boys today?

► Be the boy who is called out by the men in the Nigerian village. How do you feel as you are standing at the door with your mother? As you are walking toward the men?

► Who were the "elders" in your life when you were a boy? Talk about those who influenced you, whether relatives or men in your community and church. What kinds of role models were these men for you?

► What event of "calling out" can you point to in your life? If you can identify such an event, what was—and is—its effect on you?

► Why would Eli call Samuel "my son"? Have you ever been called "son" by a man who was not your father? Or do you do that with young men who are not your literal sons? What meanings and feelings are wrapped up in this for you?

PRAYER MOMENTS

Spend some time going around the circle, naming specific prayer needs. Use the Prayer Record on pages 58–62 to jot notes. Then, choose a prayer method below.

___One man prays, covering issues and concerns raised.

___Everyone prays for the man on his right.

___Pray sentence prayers, with a person designated to close.

___Focus on one key concern of the group or a group member, and all pray about that concern.

___Spend some moments in silent prayer.

___Assign specific prayer subjects to people before bowing for prayer.

___Lay hands on a brother who expresses need, and focus on that man's situation.

___Sing the doxology, or a praise chorus.

___Other method:

SUGGESTION FOR THE WEEK AHEAD

In your quiet time this week, prayerfully consider: *Is there any rite of passage in the discipleship of boys-to-men in my own church?* Plan to talk with a few other men about possible programs that could be implemented in your church along this line. (For example: How about an annual Men/Teens retreat? What kinds of calling and mentoring could be done on such a retreat?)

Filling the "Hero Vacuum"

CHECK-IN / UPDATE

What's happening with you?
► A feeling to report
► A problem or struggle to share
► A personal or spiritual growth question/insight
► A summary of your week: issues/concerns/joys
► A progress report/accountability check

ONE MAN'S STORY

Mitchell and I had become close friends. Since he was quarterback of the seventh-grade football team, we had to spend time together. (You know the bit—the player has to think like the coach.) Those times became precious for both of us. We liked each other. We had some of the same values. We enjoyed each others' sense of duty. Mitchell was a very mature, responsible, well-adjusted seventh-grader who was fun to be around—the kind of boy who just had to be a source of joy for his parents.

After football season, even though I only saw Mitchell during class and occasionally in the halls, he was still one of my closest friends. But as winter wore on and both of us got busy, our relationship waned some. I did notice that Mitchell wasn't as jovial in class as he had been, and some of his work wasn't as good as I expected; but I attributed that to snow depression. (As a native Southwesterner, I can understand such things.)

My first cause for alarm came in mid-January. I was called into the office to help the principal with a delicate matter. Mitchell had been caught fighting in the bathroom. Instead of meeting the witty, easygoing, controlled young man I had grown to appreciate, I discovered a calloused, angry person. I could tell that this wasn't a passing mood. Very subtly, there had been a change in his personality, almost a reversal. I decided to interfere, so I called his father. A couple of days later, we met. The father told me about his separation and impending divorce, and he asked for my help during this difficult period. I promised to do what I could.

But as soon as the father reported the conversation to Mitchell, I lost my best friend. That boy sat in class and glared at me. When I turned my back, he made snide remarks under his breath. He approached his assignments with an apathy that looked like resentment.

What had I done to him to earn that kind of treatment? I had entered his secret temple. I had discovered his vulnerability. I knew something about him that he had been trying so hard to hide, and he hated me for it. . . .

I think his hurt went even deeper. . . . At a time when Mitchell was trying to define the meaning of being a man, the one man he had decided to use as a model deserted him. *That vacuum, once created, had to be filled with something.*

—Cliff Schimmels[6]

**Superman and Batman are currently unavailable.
Will Arthur Bagley do?**

GOD ENTERS THE STORY

The king asked, "Is there no one still left of the house of Saul to whom I can show God's kindness?"

Ziba answered the king, "There is still a son of Jonathan; he is crippled in both feet."

"Where is he?" the king asked.

19

Ziba answered, "He is at the house of Makir son of Ammiel in Lo Debar." So King David had him brought from Lo Debar, from the house of Makir son of Ammiel. When Mephibosheth son of Jonathan, the son of Saul, came to David, he bowed down to pay him honor.

David said, "Mephibosheth!"

"Your servant," he replied.

"Don't be afraid," David said to him, "for I will surely show you kindness for the sake of your father Jonathan. I will restore to you all the land that belonged to your grandfather Saul, and you will always eat at my table."

Mephibosheth bowed down and said, "What is your servant, that you should notice a dead dog like me?"

Then the king summoned Ziba, Saul's servant, and said to him, "I have given your master's grandson everything that belonged to Saul and his family. You and your sons and your servants are to farm the land for him and bring in the crops, so that your master's grandson may be provided for. And Mephibosheth, grandson of your master, will always eat at my table." (Now Ziba had fifteen sons and twenty servants.)

Then Ziba said to the king, "Your servant will do whatever my lord the king commands his servant to do." So Mephibosheth ate at David's table like one of the king's sons. Mephibosheth had a young son named Mica, and all the members of Ziba's household were servants of Mephibosheth. And Mephibosheth lived in Jerusalem, because he always ate at the king's table, and he was crippled in both feet.

— *2 Samuel 9:3-13*

Join with others in following my example, brothers, and take note of those who live according to the pattern we gave you.

—*Philippians 3:17*

THE STORY IN QUOTES

Americans are living in a post-heroic age, where young adults are much less likely than their parents to have role models. A survey by Scripps Howard News Service and Ohio University shows that 60 percent of adults have no heroes. Of those who do have heroes, most said their heroes are either dead or are historical figures.

Defining "hero" as anyone with admirable courage (other than family or biblical figures), the study revealed that the last thirty or forty years has been a time of extreme cynicism toward heroes, in which a media-wise culture has witnessed the debunking and demythologizing of one so-called hero after another.

It's not a healthy trend, according to former U.S. Education Secretary William Bennett, author of the best-seller *The Book of Virtues:* "It is particularly important for young people to have heroes. This is a way to teach them by moral example, so that we can point to someone as an ideal." Maybe they should include biblical figures in their next survey.

—*in* New Man *magazine*[7]

In order to influence a child, one must be careful not to be that child's parent or grandparent.

—*Don Marquis*[8]

CAN YOU RELATE?

► Which one of the three story-sections above "rang a bell" with you? How?

► What personal story or experience comes to mind, in relation to these themes: (a) **the lack of heroes in society, and/or in your life;** or (b) **the possibility of filling the "hero vacuum" for someone else?**

► What other **insights** came to the surface for you? What **questions** were raised in your mind? Do you have any **personal applications** to consider?

► What else would you like to say (if you are in a group) about this topic?

FOR FURTHER THOUGHT OR DISCUSSION

► Who was the "one man" who deserted Mitchell? If you are divorced—or come from a broken family—how does the story of Mitchell affect you?

► Who were your heroes as a boy? Who are some of your heroes today? Do you agree that "Americans are living in a post-heroic age"? What evidence can you offer to support your view?

► In what ways was King David a hero in Mephibosheth's life? Name some of the character qualities that likely spurred David to reach out to the younger man.

► What would it mean, in practical terms, to "show kindness" (as David did) to a younger man today?

► In light of the biblical story, what would you say is the effect on self-esteem for anyone who receives a hero's attention? Can you give an example from your own life?

► Look again at the wry quote by Don Marquis. What truth is there in the idea that a nonparent might have a special kind of influence that eludes the parents themselves? When have you seen this principle in action?

► If God were to call you to be a "coach" in a similar manner as Cliff Schimmels, who would be a prime candidate for your mentoring efforts?

PRAYER MOMENTS

Spend some time going around the circle, naming specific prayer needs. Use the Prayer Record on pages 58–62 to jot notes. Then, choose a prayer method below.

___One man prays, covering issues and concerns raised.

___Everyone prays for the man on his right.

___Pray sentence prayers, with a person designated to close.

___Focus on one key concern of the group or a group member, and all pray about that concern.

___Spend some moments in silent prayer.

___Assign specific prayer subjects to people before bowing for prayer.

___Lay hands on a brother who expresses need, and focus on that man's situation.

___Sing the doxology, or a praise chorus.

___Other method:

SUGGESTION FOR THE WEEK AHEAD

At some point during the week, do an exercise that will help you answer this question:

What would it take for me to reach a point of being able to say with the Apostle Paul, "Follow my example"? (See Philippians 3:17.)

First read Ephesians 4:22-24, and then jot these two column headings on a sheet of paper:

Things to Put Off   *Things to Put On*

Write some practical entries in each column, listing lifestyle changes that would move you closer to becoming a "pattern" for others to follow.

Envision This!

What's happening with you?
- A feeling to report
- A problem or struggle to share
- A personal or spiritual growth question/insight
- A summary of your week: issues/concerns/joys
- A progress report/accountability check

ONE MAN'S STORY

He had a bushy shock of white hair—and his unusual name only highlighted it: Rev. Forest Bush. He was my first mentor in ministry, and to me that white hair stood for exactly what it has traditionally come to symbolize: wisdom.

I was young, just out of Bible school, not even started into seminary. But this wise conference pastor saw me as capable, apparently believing that my early twenty-something enthusiasm would offset whatever I still lacked in formal training.

I was to take a tiny church on partial pay and continue with seminary after a couple of years "in the trenches." And I did, indeed, approach the task with all the vigor and idealism I could muster . . . before soon slipping deeply into the mire of discouragement.

The thing I remember about Forest, though, was that in his visits or in our phone conversations, he was always accepting, gently encouraging, constantly telling me how things would be as soon as we "turned the corner" with the church. After six months, when I phoned to report that not one single new member had yet entered the church—and I was horrified at my apparent pastoral failure—he was not in the least disturbed. "Just keep on loving those people," he said. "They have so much talent and ability; let them use it." As far as he was concerned, this little church would be a great one before too long . . . he could virtually see it.

Amazingly, I began to see it too. I caught his vision as though it had been a baseball tossed from his mitt to mine. Why did I begin to put so much stock in the words of this man who was decades my senior? For one thing, while "house sitting" his home one evening I came across a scrapbook on his bookshelf. I opened it to an old snapshot of Forest as a young pastor, probably about my age at the time. Was he standing in a pulpit preaching to a tiny flock? No. Was he presiding over a wedding or a funeral? No, not in the one old Polaroid that has left such an impression in my mind all these years. Instead, there was Forest atop a bulldozer, triumphant smile on his face, mounds of broken-up mortar, bricks, boards, and shingles cluttering the background. That rubble had once housed the blossoming numbers of his first pastorate, a congregation which—as he told me later—had far outgrown its old building under brand-new sermons.

It was everything I needed to keep going. Rev. Bush had been there, he knew what could happen. He had been a part of it, happily bulldozing old bricks while claiming new vistas for the Lord. And the vision he gave me was the glimpse of a future

so sure and so certain that I felt I could reach out and touch it. It was like broken plaster and bits of torn-up carpet in the palm of my hand.
—*Gary Wilde*

GOD ENTERS THE STORY

Where there is no vision, the people perish.
—*Proverbs 29:18*

The next day Moses took his seat to serve as judge for the people, and they stood around him from morning till evening. When his father-in-law saw all that Moses was doing for the people, he said, "What is this you are doing for the people? Why do you alone sit as judge, while all these people stand around you from morning till evening?"

Moses answered him, "Because the people come to me to seek God's will. Whenever they have a dispute, it is brought to me, and I decide between the parties and inform them of God's decrees and laws." Moses' father-in-law replied, "What you are doing is not good. You and these people who come to you will only wear yourselves out. The work is too heavy for you; you cannot handle it alone. Listen now to me and I will give you some advice, and may God be with you. You must be the people's representative before God and bring their disputes to Him. Teach them the decrees and laws, and show them the way to live and the duties they are to perform. But select capable men from all the people—men who fear God, trustworthy men who hate dishonest gain—and appoint them as officials over thousands, hundreds, fifties and tens. Have them serve as judges for the people at all times, but have them bring every difficult case to you; the simple cases they can decide themselves. That will make your load lighter, because they will share it with you. If you do this and God so commands, you will be able to stand the strain, and all these people will go home satisfied."

Moses listened to his father-in-law and did everything he said.
—*Exodus 18:13-24*

THE STORY IN QUOTES

The visions that we present to our [younger generation] shape the future. They become self-fulfilling prophecies. Dreams are maps.
—*Carl Sagan*[9]

Moses was empowered, as he took his father-in-law's advice and applied it immediately. Thank God for wise and timely counsel. Not only was Moses relieved and more effective in his responsibilities, but the people and his family were blessed as well. I'm sure Moses learned to check periodically with his father-in-law . . . hopefully before committing himself to any future action.

We all are responsible to God for our own decisions and to discern His will, but we are foolish to *not* take advantage of the experiences and wisdom of others in the process.
—*Paul D. Stanley and J. Robert Clinton*[10]

You may see your teen writing notes in youth group or making spit wads in church. He may fight with his brothers and sisters at home. You may wonder how your teen could change the world when you can't even get him to change his sheets. God sees all that stuff too, yet He still believes in his potential—and He is still counting on him.

Our young people need to know we have discovered the seeds of greatness within them. When they finally find someone who recognizes their potential, they will abandon the direction this world has given them. When they see an older generation that is convinced of their potential, there is nothing they won't do to fulfill that potential.
—*Ron Luce*[11]

The tenders of vision are often lonely, usually unpopular, and frequently demand that others change. People with a vision inject ambiguity and risk and uncertainty into our lives.

—*Max DePree* [12]

CAN YOU RELATE?

► Which one of the three story-sections above "rang a bell" with you? How?

► What personal story or experience comes to mind, in relation to these themes: (a) **the call to offer and nurture a "vision" to younger men;** or (b) **being grasped by a mentor's vision?**

► What other **insights** came to the surface for you? What **questions** were raised in your mind? Do you have any **personal applications** to consider?

► What else would you like to say (if you are in a group) about this topic?

FOR FURTHER THOUGHT OR DISCUSSION

► When were you provided vision from someone older and wiser than you?

► How would you summarize the vision that Moses' father-in-law gave to Moses in Exodus 18?

► In your opinion, what does it take for a leader or mentor to be able to convey a vision? What is required of the man who is being mentored?

► Why would it be important to a mentoring relationship that there be a vision at its center? Would this vision need to be explicit and spoken? Explain.

► Look at the statement by Carl Sagan. How is the theme of this session like, and unlike, the idea of a "self-fulfilling prophecy"?

► What do you think Max DePree meant by saying that people with vision "inject ambiguity and risk and uncertainty into our lives"?

PRAYER MOMENTS

Spend some time going around the circle, naming specific prayer needs. Use the Prayer Record on pages 58–62 to jot notes. Then, choose a prayer method below.

___One man prays, covering issues and concerns raised.
___Everyone prays for the man on his right.
___Pray sentence prayers, with a person designated to close.
___Focus on one key concern of the group or a group member, and all pray about that concern.
___Spend some moments in silent prayer.
___Assign specific prayer subjects to people before bowing for prayer.
___Lay hands on a brother who expresses need, and focus on that man's situation.
___Sing the doxology, or a praise chorus.
___Other method:

SUGGESTION FOR THE WEEK AHEAD

During your quiet time, take a moment to think about the importance of vision. In your journal jot the name of a young man in whom you see potential—either in the work environment or in Christian discipleship. Then do two things: (1) determine to pray frequently for this man; and (2) ask God for an opportunity to let this man know what you see in him.

Demonstrate It

CHECK-IN / UPDATE

What's happening with you?

- A feeling to report
- A problem or struggle to share
- A personal or spiritual growth question/insight
- A summary of your week: issues/concerns/joys
- A progress report/accountability check

ONE MAN'S STORY

My dad died last night.

He left like he had lived. Quietly. Graciously. With dignity. Without demands or harsh words or even a frown, he surrendered himself—a tired, frail, humble gentleman—into the waiting arms of his Savior. Death, selfish and cursed enemy of man, won another battle.

As I stroked the hair from his forehead and kissed him good-bye, a hundred boyhood memories played around in my head.

➤ When I learned to ride a bike, he was there.

➤ When I wrestled with the multiplication tables, his quick wit erased the hassle.

➤ When I discovered the adventure of driving a car, he was near, encouraging me.

➤ When I got my first job (delivering newspapers), he informed me how to increase my subscriptions and win the prize. It worked!

➤ When I mentioned a young woman I had fallen in love with, he pulled me aside and talked straight about being responsible for her welfare and happiness.

➤ When I did a hitch in the Marine Corps, the discipline I had learned from him made the transition easier. . . .

Last night I realized I had him to thank for my deep love for America. And for knowing how to tenderly care for my wife. And for laughing at impossibilities. And for some of the habits I have picked up, like approaching people with a positive spirit rather than a negative one, staying with a task until it is finished, taking good care of my personal belongings, keeping my shoes shined, speaking up rather than mumbling, respecting authority, and standing alone (if necessary) in support of my personal convictions rather than giving in to more popular opinion. For these things I am deeply indebted to the man who raised me.

Admittedly, much of my dad's instruction was indirect—by model rather than by explicit statement. *I do not recall his overt declarations of love as clearly as I do his demonstrations of it. . . .* He leaves in his legacy a well-marked Bible I treasure, a series of feelings that I need to deepen my roots, and a thousand memories that comfort me as I replace denial with acceptance and praise.

—Charles R. Swindoll[13]

PORTLEYK

Tommy, I'd love to go to the video arcade with you today, but my dad is going to teach me how to build my house on rock instead of sand.

GOD ENTERS THE STORY

Only be careful, and watch yourselves closely so that you do not forget the things your eyes have seen or let them slip from your heart as long as you live. Teach them to your children and to their children after them. Remember the day you stood before the Lord your God at Horeb, when He said to me, "Assemble the people before Me to hear My words so that they may learn to revere Me as long as they live in the land and may teach them to their children."...

"These commandments that I give you today are to be upon your hearts. Impress them on your children. Talk about them

when you sit at home and when you walk along the road, when you lie down and when you get up. Tie them as symbols on your hands and bind them on your foreheads. Write them on the doorframes of your houses and on your gates."
—*Deuteronomy 4:9-10; 6:6-8*

When the time drew near for David to die, he gave a charge to Solomon his son. "I am about to go the way of all the earth," he said. "So be strong, show yourself a man, and observe what the Lord your God requires: Walk in His ways, and keep his decrees and commands, His laws and requirements, as written in the Law of Moses, so that you may prosper in all you do and wherever you go, and that the Lord may keep His promise to me: 'If your descendants watch how they live, and if they walk faithfully before Me with all their heart and soul, you will never fail to have a man on the throne of Israel.'"
—*1 Kings 2:1-4*

I tell you the truth, the Son can do nothing by Himself; He can do only what He sees His Father doing, because whatever the Father does the Son also does. For the Father loves the Son and shows Him all He does.
—*John 5:19-20*

THE STORY IN QUOTES

An important thing for parents to teach their children is how to get along without them.
—*Frances Clark*[14]

My son wanted to help change a flat tire on my car. He couldn't loosen the lug nuts. He ran out of energy to unscrew them all. He couldn't lift the old tire off or put the new one on. Once the new tire was on, he tried to get away with only putting on every other lug nut. It took twice as long with his help.

While he couldn't help me as much as he thought he could, he went away thinking he had helped me more than he did. The experience made a large spiritual impression on him. His self-esteem grew by a mile, and now he understands the concepts of diligence and excellence in a deeper way. Those are biblical values, and I impressed them upon my son in a way that was natural, not contrived. I wasn't teaching him how to change a flat tire; I was teaching him how to be a man of God.

—*Patrick Morley*[15]

I talk and talk, and I haven't taught people in fifty years what my father taught by example in one week.

—*Mario Cuomo*[16]

CAN YOU RELATE?

► Which one of the three story-sections above "rang a bell" with you? How?

► What personal story or experience comes to mind, in relation to these themes: (a) **mentoring your children;** or (b) **benefiting—or not—from the legacy of your own father?**

► What other **insights** came to the surface for you? What **questions** were raised in your mind? Do you have any **personal applications** to consider?

► What else would you like to say (if you are in a group) about this topic?

FOR FURTHER THOUGHT OR DISCUSSION

► How seriously did your father take his responsibility for mentoring his own children? How did he demonstrate that he was aware—or not aware—of that responsibility?

► If you never knew your father (or only knew him for a short time), how does this loss affect your life today?

► Focus on the quotation by Frances Clark. If you have children, calculate their ability to get along without you: now; five years from now; fifteen years from now. What part have you played in their preparation for your potential absence?

► What did you learn from your dad—or another man—that was conveyed mostly without words? What scene comes to mind?

► When have you been surprised to find that a younger person was watching you closely as a "closet mentoree"? Do you think we need more, or less, awareness of the secret watchers?

► In the Deuteronomy passage, what aspects of "informal" teaching could you directly apply to your life today? Share some practical examples.

► Name some of your personal qualities about which a close relative might say: "That's just the way your father was." Are these qualities a blessing or a burden to you? Why?

PRAYER MOMENTS

Spend some time going around the circle, naming specific prayer needs. Use the Prayer Record on pages 58–62 to jot notes. Then, choose a prayer method below.

___One man prays, covering issues and concerns raised.

___Everyone prays for the man on his right.

___Pray sentence prayers, with a person designated to close.

___Focus on one key concern of the group or a group member, and all pray about that concern.

___Spend some moments in silent prayer.

___Assign specific prayer subjects to people before bowing for prayer.

___Lay hands on a brother who expresses need, and focus on that man's situation.

___Sing the doxology, or a praise chorus.
___Other method:

SUGGESTION FOR THE WEEK AHEAD

Meditate for a few minutes on the Frances Clark quotation. Then, if you have children, draw up a list of Top Five things (knowledge, skills, character traits) that you would want to impart to your children—*assuming you have one year left to live*. Make practical plans to start conveying these things intentionally, beginning today!

If you do not have children, prayerfully consider:

What was I given by my father that prepared me for life without him? (Offer a prayer of thanksgiving to God for these things.)

Or:

What do I wish my father had given me in preparation for his absence? (Share your hurt or frustration with God in a moment of prayer.)

Multiplying Ministry

CHECK-IN / UPDATE

What's happening with you?

- ▶ A feeling to report
- ▶ A problem or struggle to share
- ▶ A personal or spiritual growth question/insight
- ▶ A summary of your week: issues/concerns/joys
- ▶ A progress report/accountability check

ONE MAN'S STORY

It happened in the church hallway. Harold personally challenged me to join a special, six-week-long small group that would explore some basic concepts for Christians who wanted to grow. The invitation appealed to me and yet frightened me. But put on the spot, and not able to think of a reason why I should not join, I agreed.

From a distance I had been attracted to Harold. He was serious about following Christ, and I sensed he knew some things that could help me. I later learned that he had been a believer for only three years. But those years involved steady, solid spiritual growth under the watchful eye of a mature Air Force sergeant. Harold had transferred from Europe to Japan because he had heard the poker was better there. But in Japan, Christ—not cards—dominated his life. He saw some radical Christians who lived out their commitments openly before their fellow servicemen....

Harold did several things that impressed me. He showed us that he was personally concerned for each person in the group. He challenged us with practical assignments that affected our daily lives—assignments that later we could use with others in the same way he used them with us. He sought to go beyond the time we met as a group and spent personal time with us outside of the small-group setting....

During the small group sessions I began to sense that Harold had more that he could give to me that would aid me in my Christian walk. He invited me to meet with him individually on a regular basis. I responded. I learned much. But most of all, we established a relationship. Though we have since lived in various parts of the United States and the world, God has repeatedly intertwined our lives at crucial decision times. Sometimes our contact was prolonged and we picked up where we had left off. At other times it was momentary and resulted in wise counsel that confirmed or clarified God's guidance.

Our relationship is mutually stimulating. I never think of Harold without whispering Philippians 1:3, for I know he was sent by God for that brief interlude that started me on a life of discipleship.

—J. Robert Clinton[17]

GOD ENTERS THE STORY

As iron sharpens iron, so one man sharpens another.

—Proverbs 27:17

Then the Lord told [Elijah], "Go back by the desert road to Damascus, and when you arrive, anoint Hazael to be king of Syria. Then anoint Jehu (son of Nimshi) to be king of Israel, and anoint Elisha (the son of Shaphat of Abel-meholah) to replace you as My prophet...

So Elijah went and found Elisha who was plowing a field with eleven other teams ahead of him; he was at the end of the line with the last team. Elijah went over to him and threw his coat across his shoulders and walked away again.

Elisha left the oxen standing there and ran after Elijah and said to him, "First let me go and say good-bye to my father and mother, and then I'll go with you!"

Elijah replied, "Go on back! Why all the excitement?"

Elisha then returned to his oxen, killed them, and used wood from the plow to build a fire to roast their flesh. He passed around the meat to the other plowmen, and they all had a great feast. Then he went with Elijah, as his assistant.

—*1 Kings 19:15-16, 19-21 (TLB)*

So the Lord said to Moses, "Take Joshua son of Nun, a man in whom is the spirit, and lay your hand on him. Have him stand before Eleazar the priest and the entire assembly and commission him in their presence. Give him some of your authority so the whole Israelite community will obey him."

—*Numbers 27:18-20*

As Jesus was walking beside the Sea of Galilee, He saw two brothers, Simon called Peter and his brother Andrew. They were casting a net into the lake, for they were fishermen. "Come, follow Me," Jesus said, "and I will make you fishers of men." At once they left their nets and followed him. Going on from there, He saw two other brothers, James son of Zebedee and his brother John. They were in a boat with their father Zebedee, preparing their nets. Jesus called them, and immediately they left the boat and their father and followed Him.

—*Matthew 4:18-22*

You then, my son, be strong in the grace that is in Christ Jesus. And the things you have heard me say in the presence of many witnesses entrust to reliable men who will also be qualified to teach others.

—*2 Timothy 2:1-2*

THE STORY IN QUOTES

Moses trained Joshua to take his place, so that Moses might become dispensable. So did Jesus train His disciples versus His ascension. So should all useful persons train others to take their place. Success without a successor is failure.[18]

The noncom's first order caught us off guard. He told us to find a buddy. Some of us would have preferred the cliff. "This is step one," he growled. "You need to find yourself a Ranger buddy. You will stick together. You will never leave each other. You will encourage each other, and, as necessary, you will carry each other." It was the Army's way of saying, "*Difficult assignments require a friend. Together is better. You need someone to help you accomplish the tough course ahead.*"

—*Stu Weber* [19]

In only three years Christ defined a mission and formed strategies to carry it out. With a staff of 12 unlikely men, He organized Christianity, which today has branches in all the world's countries and a 32.4 percent share of the world's population, twice as big as its nearest rival. Managers want to develop people to their full potential, taking ordinary people and making them extraordinary. This is what Christ did with His disciples. Jesus was the most effective executive in history. The results He achieved are second to none.

—*James Hind* [20]

Lucy: Do you think anybody ever really changes?

Linus: I've changed a lot in the last year.

Lucy: I mean for the better.

—*Charles Schulz* [21]

CAN YOU RELATE?

► Which one of the three story-sections above "rang a bell" with you? How?

► What personal story or experience comes to mind, in relation to these themes: (a) **discipling one another in the Christian life;** or (b) **mentoring a successor?**

► What other **insights** came to the surface for you? What **questions** were raised in your mind? Do you have any **personal applications** to consider?

► What else would you like to say (if you are in a group) about this topic?

FOR FURTHER THOUGHT OR DISCUSSION

► Robert Clinton speaks of being "frightened" by the prospect of meeting regularly with another man in a discipling relationship. How would you describe that kind of fear? In your opinion, what are some of its causes?

► How do you feel about being given "practical assignments" from another man for spiritual growth? Could you envision yourself doing this? Why, or why not?

► Elijah was supposed to find a replacement for himself (see 1 Kings 19:16). But Elisha became Elijah's "assistant" first (see v. 21). When have you seen training operating in similar fashion in the workplace? What is the wisdom in this method?

► Focus on Numbers 27:20 and the fact that Moses was instructed to give Joshua some of his authority. Would you agree that "giving away power" should be a part of any mentoring relationship? Explain.

► How does 2 Timothy 2:1-2 remind you of multiplication?

► Is it true that "success without a successor is a failure"? Who do you know that has failed in this way? How successful do you think you will be at the end of your term?

PRAYER MOMENTS

Spend some time going around the circle, naming specific prayer needs. Use the Prayer Record on pages 58–62 to jot notes. Then, choose a prayer method below.

___One man prays, covering issues and concerns raised.

___Everyone prays for the man on his right.

___Pray sentence prayers, with a person designated to close.

___Focus on one key concern of the group or a group member, and all pray about that concern.

___Spend some moments in silent prayer.

___Assign specific prayer subjects to people before bowing for prayer.

___Lay hands on a brother who expresses need, and focus on that man's situation.

___Sing the doxology, or a praise chorus.

___Other method:

SUGGESTION FOR THE WEEK AHEAD

During your quiet time this week, think about Jesus being called an "executive" by James Hind. On a page of your journal, list some Top Executive Qualities that you see in Jesus. Find Scripture passages that illustrate your ideas, then take some time to meditate on those passages during the days ahead.

To Open . . . Or Not?

Check-in / Update

What's happening with you?
- A feeling to report
- A problem or struggle to share
- A personal or spiritual growth question/insight
- A summary of your week: issues/concerns/joys
- A progress report/accountability check

One Man's Story

I was in the car with Phil when he suddenly pulled to the curb, apparently wanting to talk. I was glad, because as a young pastor I wanted to develop a mentoring relationship with this college student. Accepting a ride from him seemed to be the opening for significant conversation.

But he surprised me by blurting a little speech, reeling off the words as though previously memorized: "Gary, I'm usually kind of nervous in relating with people, afraid of what they'll think of me, but I have a theory that if I tell a person—right off—the absolute worst thing about me, then I can relax and be free because I'll have nothing to hide from then on."

I was just beginning to reply that it was an interesting concept when he broke in with: "Well, here goes. Anyway, I have this problem with sexual lust, see, I secretly buy a lot of those skin magazines and spend lots of time fantasizing, then I throw 'em away and buy some more. It actually gets pretty expensive, though I suppose you wouldn't think about me that way, but it's the truth and nobody knows it, I mean, except for you, now."

He smiled at me triumphantly because a big load was off his chest and he was presumably now "free" not to worry about what I thought of him. The shocker came in my realization that it was now supposed to be my turn! With expectant eyes drilling into mine, everything in his body language beckoned: "OK, go.... So what's the absolute worst, Gary? I can handle it. Go ahead."

I chickened out. Actually, I could have told any number of true, down-to-earth stories of similar struggles with lust—and a few other not-so-nice peccadillos. But, after all, I was his spiritual leader. *And where does he get off thinking that I too am some kind of gross sinner?*

I said something appropriately pastoral: "That's good, Phil, being able to share with me like that; it took some courage, I'll be praying for you." Or something like that. When you offer a proper generalization in these situations, the words don't really matter; what matters is that you shut down the dialogue, close off the relationship—quick.

Should I have opened up to Phil with a reciprocal level of transparency?

I played it a bit holier than that. The thing is, I can't remember another significant talk with the young man during the rest of my years in that church.

—Gary Wilde

GOD ENTERS THE STORY

You, then, who teach others, do you not teach yourself? You who preach against stealing, do you steal? You who say that people should not commit adultery, do you commit adultery? You who abhor idols, do you rob temples? You who brag about the law, do you dishonor God by breaking the law?
—*Romans 2:21-23*

Who is weak, and I do not feel weak? Who is led into sin, and I do not inwardly burn? If I must boast, I will boast of the things that show my weakness. The God and Father of the Lord Jesus, who is to be praised forever, knows that I am not lying.
—*2 Corinthians 11:29-31*

For the appeal we make does not spring from error or impure motives, nor are we trying to trick you. On the contrary, we speak as men approved by God to be entrusted with the Gospel. We are not trying to please men but God, who tests our hearts. You know we never used flattery, nor did we put on a mask to cover up greed—God is our witness.

We were not looking for praise from men, not from you or anyone else. As apostles of Christ we could have been a burden to you, but we were gentle among you, like a mother caring for her little children. We loved you so much that we were delighted to share with you not only the gospel of God but our lives as well, because you had become so dear to us.
—*1 Thessalonians 2:3-8*

Here is a trustworthy saying that deserves full acceptance: Christ Jesus came into the world to save sinners—of whom I am the worst. But for that very reason I was shown mercy so that in me, the worst of sinners, Christ Jesus might display His unlimited patience as an example for those who would believe on Him and receive eternal life.

—1 Timothy 1:15-16

THE STORY IN QUOTES

I am sure my readers understand the subtle temptation which assails me: that of trying to be the personage I am expected to be. It slips in disguised as an honest concern for the proper fulfillment of my vocation.... In order not to disappoint them I ought to tell them only of my positive experiences. In fact they are always disconcerted at first when I speak of my own difficulties, doubts and failings. But they soon come to see that this atmosphere of truth brings us closer and binds us together. My experience of the power of God means more to them than it would if they thought me a quite different sort of person from themselves.

—Paul Tournier [22]

How often we hide behind masks and hug delusions with compulsive passion because we are afraid to be known, to be loved—but in the nearness of real, deep, substantial love we run back to our masks of isolation, shallowness, and safety in terror of being revealed and accepted. We hide ourselves in acts of passion; we buy love under false prudence; we substitute biological pleasures for the divine wonder and peril of love; we surround ourselves with cold, icy barriers to defend the smug self from being shattered by love.

—William McNamara [23]

All men are frauds. The only difference between them is that some admit it. I myself deny it.

—H.L. Mencken [24]

CAN YOU RELATE?

► Which one of the three story-sections above "rang a bell" with you? How?

► What personal story or experience comes to mind, in relation to this theme: **the importance of genuineness and transparency in a mentoring relationship?**

► What other **insights** came to the surface for you? What **questions** were raised in your mind? Do you have any **personal applications** to consider?

► What else would you like to say (if you are in a group) about this topic?

FOR FURTHER THOUGHT OR DISCUSSION

► If you could have "stopped the camera" in the scene right after Phil's revelations, what principles or guidelines would you have offered Gary Wilde—as to how he should respond?

► How do you, personally, decide who is "safe," and who isn't, for a deeper level of vulnerability in friendship with another Christian? In a mentoring relationship?

► Where do you draw the line between legitimate sharing of personal struggles and inappropriate "airing of dirty laundry"?

► On a scale of 1 to 5, how self-revealing would you say the Apostle Paul was in the God's Story Scriptures (see also Romans 7:14-25)?

► Look again at the statement by Paul Tournier. He says that an "atmosphere of truth brings us closer and binds us together." Do you agree? If so, when have you seen this principle in action?

► In your opinion, do our spiritual leaders (pastors, denominational executives, ministry heads, etc.) need to be MORE OPEN, or LESS OPEN, about their spiritual struggles? How does your own pastor approach this issue?

PRAYER MOMENTS

Spend some time going around the circle, naming specific prayer needs. Use the Prayer Record on pages 58–62 to jot notes. Then, choose a prayer method below.

___One man prays, covering issues and concerns raised.
___Everyone prays for the man on his right.
___Pray sentence prayers, with a person designated to close.
___Focus on one key concern of the group or a group member, and all pray about that concern.
___Spend some moments in silent prayer.
___Assign specific prayer subjects to people before bowing for prayer.
___Lay hands on a brother who expresses need, and focus on that man's situation.
___Sing the doxology, or a praise chorus.
___Other method:

SUGGESTION FOR THE WEEK AHEAD

During the coming week, plan to call another man who has attended your group meetings. Try to pick one of the men that you know the least. Have a brief discussion about what happened during the course of your six sessions on mentoring. You might talk about such things as:
► How did you like the course?
► Did you make any new friends?
► What things did you learn?

► What challenged you?
► How have your views, goals, priorities been affected?

You might round out your conversation by sharing ongoing prayer needs and exploring potential fellowship opportunities for the future.

Group Strengtheners

Draw on the following resources to deepen the fellowship in your group, both in the meeting and during the week.

CREATIVE SESSION STARTERS

Here are some creative ideas to help you launch into the topic of each session. For some sessions you'll just immediately start with discussion, but other times you may want to use one of these more active starter ideas. A few days in advance, read through the suggestion below for your week and decide if it would spark interest and discussion in your group. Feel free to adapt the ideas to the size and setting of your group. It's your call!

For Session 1

If your group is new, and many of the men do not know each other, use this first activity as a get-acquainted exercise. Ask all the men to stand and gather in a line from oldest to youngest—but the catch is that "age" is based on this formula:

Oldest = having the most life-lessons to GIVE
Youngest = having the most life-lessons to LEARN

Tell the men to discuss among themselves as they make their decisions about where to stand. When a line is formed, introduce the theme of this study course by saying: "We'll be considering the concept of mentoring, or discipleship. It involves many ideas, including the call to bring boys into manhood, to disciple our children, to befriend and instruct others in the faith, and to become a leader in our community and church. Underlying it all is the idea that we have wisdom to convey and to learn from one another. Typically, it is the more experienced, probably older men who have knowledge and skills to impart to the younger generation."

Now have everyone sit down and give each man an opportunity to answer one of these questions (jot on chalkboard or newsprint, if possible):

► *An aspect of "life wisdom" that I might be able
    to convey to another man is. . . .*

► *An aspect of "life wisdom" that I'd like
    to gain from another man is. . . .*

Stress that responses do not have to be on a grand scale, but can be simple and practical. For example, one man may say that he could tell about what keeps a marriage together for thirty-five years. A younger man might learn from a seasoned executive about making career-move decisions. After a few minutes of sharing, move into One Man's Story.

For Session 2
Have your group members form pairs to talk about an imaginary event. Say: "Imagine being invited to dinner with your 'biggest hero' (whether living or dead—but not Jesus!)." Tell the partners that they should share their responses to these ques-

tions, related to their imaginary hero-dinner: (1) Who would your host be? (2) What one burning question would you want to ask, in order to learn the most from your hero? (3) What activity would you choose, if your hero invited you to spend the next afternoon together?

Allow sufficient time for partners to report to the whole group about their responses. Then move into your session, perhaps focusing first on the biblical story of Mephibosheth dining at the king's table.

For Session 3

Begin by handing each man an index card and a pencil. Tell the men that their task is to jot a response to this statement: "What I wanted to be when I grew up." Have them jot just one occupation, which was a goal either from their childhood or their adolescent years.

Gather the cards in a pile, shuffle them, and read them aloud, one at a time. After each one, have the whole group guess whose card you are reading.

There may be some interesting surprises! Some men may have had a very early vision of themselves in a particular career and pursued it from an early age. Others may have "landed" in a completely different kind of life than they envisioned.

When all the cards' writers have been guessed, briefly discuss this question before launching into your session:

How important has it been to you in your career (or other endeavors) to have an idea of the way things would be in the future?

For Session 4

Start your session by doing a takeoff on Dave Letterman's "Stupid Human Tricks." Ask volunteers to *demonstrate* for the group a "special" talent or skill they have. Examples might include:

- ▶ being able to juggle
- ▶ touching thumb to forearm
- ▶ fitting a billiard ball in mouth

- ► blowing air out of eye sockets
- ► walking on hands
- ► touch nose with tongue
- ► Other: you name it!

Follow up your silly talent show by focusing on the quotation by Mario Cuomo. Emphasize the power of *demonstrating* discipleship as you move into your session.

For Session 5

Read aloud Proverbs 27:17 to begin your session: "As iron sharpens iron, so one man sharpens another." Ask: *When it comes to either being sharpened by, or sharpening other men, what metal are you?*

Give your men a few minutes of silence to think about what kind of metal they are. Have each man choose one of these responses and prepare to give a reason for their choice (such as the examples given):

- ► Iron ore: I'm ready to be tested and purified through accountability.
- ► Tin: I need to build a stronger character before trying to mentor others.
- ► Gold: I set the standard for some other men.
- ► Lead: I can be heavy-handed in my motivating methods.
- ► Aluminum: I'm crumpling under my own problems these days.
- ► Other:

After everyone has had a chance to share, move into your lesson's emphasis on the role of mentoring in the church.

For Session 6

Open your session with a brief Agree-Disagree exercise. Tell your men that you are going to read a series of controversial statements. After reading each one, ask for a show of hands indicating whether group members agree or disagree with the statement. Use the questions as the basis for launching into the story of Gary and Phil in One Man's Story.

Agree or Disagree?

1. We should share about our deepest struggles when asked for prayer requests.

2. It's best to keep our worst sins secret until others open up about their own worst sins.

3. There are some things about our lives that should never be divulged, even in a men's group.

4. It's a sin to act as though we have no big problems.

FELLOWSHIP DAY IDEA STARTER

A men's group can be more than just a weekly meeting. For the best results in deepening your fellowship, schedule outside activities at least once a quarter. Sample activities include doing a sports activity together or attending a special event together. With a little planning, you can make these outings into times of Christian fellowship.

This particular activity will take some advanced planning—as you meet together first to brainstorm and make your plans—for a Men/Teens Recreation Night. Plan to invite young men in your church (perhaps teens or college-age guys) to a fun event with your group. (It's up to you what the event would be, depending on the recreational opportunities in your area.)

After the event, have a brief "afterglow" time in which a few preselected men will share about some of the things they've learned regarding the importance of providing leadership and role models for boys. Especially be sure to affirm and express your blessings upon these young men. Let them know of your promise to pray for them in the days and years ahead.

Also let these boys know that they can call on any of you to talk, or to seek other forms of support (in conjunction with their parents' approval, of course). You might consider giving out a list of names and phone numbers of men who are open to phone calls from these teens.

What other creative ideas do you have for implementing the discipling principles you've discussed in your group?

VIDEO NIGHT DISCUSSION OUTLINE

Here's a suggestion for a video to watch with your group at some time during the weeks of your study course. You may wish to use the video night as a way of launching your course, or you could use it as a postcourse get-together. (Warning: This video contains an occasional coarse word. Preview it first to decide if it is appropriate for your particular group.)

Movie: *The Chosen*
- PG
- 108 minutes
- A 1981 film

What's It All About?
During World War II, Danny Saunders and Reuven Malter develop a friendship. Danny is an Orthodox Jew whose father, Reb Saunders, is the leader of a Hasidic community. Reuven's father is a liberal biblical scholar. The boys struggle to overcome cultural barriers in nurturing their friendship. Especially challenging is Reb Saunders' goal of mentoring his son into spiritual leadership as his replacement in the Hasidic community.

The Main Characters:
- Daniel: Orthodox Jewish boy with photographic memory
- Reuven: Conservative Jewish boy whose mother is dead
- Reb Saunders: Daniel's father, the rabbi leading the

Hasidic community
> ► Professor Malter: Reuven's father, a biblical scholar

General Discussion:
To what extent should a father share his dreams and goals for his children? To what extent should he "push" them to reach these goals? How much testing or challenging should a father do in order to build character in his children?

What is the role of human effort in relation to God's will? How do you view the relationship of Judaism and Christianity? (Refer to Romans 9–11, if you have time.)

Key Themes: Scenes and Quotes
Your discussion may develop more specifically around any of these numbered themes:

► **1. The idea of being groomed to take the father's/mentor's place.** Reb Saunders, leader of the Hasidic community, has dreams and goals for his son—especially that Daniel will someday take over the demanding job of spiritual leadership.

Reb. Saunders (to Reuven): He's my son! He's my most precious possession in the whole world! I mean, he takes my place afterwards. He follows me ... I don't want to lose my Danny; not my Daniel.

Discuss:
What is meant by "afterwards" here? What would it mean to "lose" Daniel? How do you relate to the idea of your own children carrying on something of your own life goals and purposes? In what ways, specifically? (Or: How have you carried on—or not—from your own father's dreams for you? How much was it evident that he wanted this to happen?)

► **2. The idea of cultivating maturity and righteousness by putting a disciple/son through testing.** Toward the end of the film, Danny's father speaks of his son's need for gaining a heart, in order to know the pain of others. Reb Saunders had used painful silence in helping his son learn compassion. Finally, he explains to Danny his purpose in it all.

Reb Saunders (to Reuven and Danny): Master of the Universe, what have you done to me? You give me a *mind* like this for a son. A *heart* I need for a son! I need for a son compassion and mercy—this I need for a son. And above all, the strength to carry pain. That I need for a son.

And how was I to do this? That was the question; how was I to teach him? How was I going to be able to do this to this son that I love—and not lose the love of my son?

I had to teach my Daniel through the wisdom—the pain—of silence . . . as my father did to me. I was forced to push him away from me. He became frightened and bewildered. But slowly he began to understand that other people in this world feel that way too. He began to understand that other people are carrying pain. And then in the silence we had between us, gradually his self-pride, his feeling of superiority, his indifference began to fade away. And he learned through the wisdom and the pain of silence *that a mind without a heart is nothing.*

So, you think that I've been cruel? Maybe. But I don't think so. Because my beloved Daniel has *learned.* I have no fear. . . because my Daniel is a *tzaddik,* a righteous man. And the world needs a righteous man.

Discuss:
How does the idea of Danny "needing a heart" relate to the opening scenes of the softball game? In your opinion, were Reb Saunders' teaching methods appropriate or too drastic? Did the end justify the means in this case? (Refer to Hebrews 12:4-13 in your response.)

▶ **3. Being wise in balancing discipline/demands with grace.**
Closing narration: There is a story in the Talmud about a king who had a son who had gone astray from his father. The son was told: "Return to your father."

The son said: "I cannot."

His father sent a messenger to say: "Return as far as you can. And I will come to you the rest of the way."

Discuss:
What is the meaning, for you, of this story that ends the film? How would you apply it in a mentoring relationship?

WEEKLY PRAYER RECORD

(Spend some time sharing prayer concerns before closing your session in prayer. Use these pages to jot some notes as others speak, then determine together the method you'll use to pray. Periodically review the record as a group to discover how prayers have been answered—or to receive updated information.)

Name	Request/Concern/Praise
_____	_____
_____	_____
_____	_____
_____	_____
_____	_____
_____	_____
_____	_____
_____	_____
_____	_____
_____	_____
_____	_____
_____	_____

Name	Request/Concern/Praise

Name	Request/Concern/Praise
_____	_____
_____	_____
_____	_____
_____	_____
_____	_____
_____	_____
_____	_____
_____	_____
_____	_____
_____	_____
_____	_____
_____	_____
_____	_____
_____	_____
_____	_____

Name	Request/Concern/Praise

Notes

1. Gordon Dalbey, *Healing the Masculine Soul* (Dallas: Word Publishing, 1988). Used by permission.

2. Robert Bly, *Iron Hans*, quoted in Gordon Dalbey, op. cit.

3. S.I. Hayakawa, cited in Lloyd Cory, ed., *Quote, Unquote* (Wheaton, Ill.: Victor Books, 1977).

4. Gordon Dalbey, *Healing the Masculine Soul*.

5. Jay Leno, cited in Robert Byrne, ed., *The Fourth and by Far the Most Recent 637 Best Things Anybody Ever Said* (New York: Fawcett Crest, 1990).

6. Cliff Schimmels, in *What Parents Try to Forget about Adolescence* (Elgin, Ill.: Life Journey Books, 1989). Used by permission.

7. Item in "Clips" section, *New Man* magazine (Lake Mary, Fla.: Strang Communications, Nov.–Dec. 1994).

8. Don Marquis, in *637 Best Things*.

9. Carl Sagan, quoted in *Growing Up Creative*, by Teresa Amabile (New York: Crown, 1989).

10. Paul D. Stanley and J. Robert Clinton, *Connecting: The Mentoring Relationships You Need to Succeed in Life* (Colorado Springs: NavPress, 1992).

11. Ron Luce, *Inspire the Fire* (Altamonte Springs, Fla.: Creation House Publishers), quoted in *New Man*, May–June 1995.

12. Max DePree, *Leadership Jazz* (New York: Dell, 1992).

13. Charles R. Swindoll, *Come Before Winter . . . And Share My Hope* (Grand Rapids: Zondervan, 1985). Used by permission.

14. Frances Clark, quoted in *Dads* (Bloomington, Minn.: Garborg's Heart 'n Home, 1993).

15. Patrick Morley, *Walking with Christ in the Details of Life* (Nashville: Thomas Nelson) as quoted in *New Man* (March–April 1995).

16. Mario Cuomo, quoted in *Dads*.

17. J. Robert Clinton, adapted from *Connecting*. Used by permission.

18. In *Quote, Unquote*.

19. Stu Weber, adapted from *Go the Distance* (in *Focus on the Family* magazine, June 1996).

20. James Hind, in the December issue of *Life* (quoted in *New Man*, March–April 1995).

21. Charles Schulz, in *637 Best Things*.

22. Paul Tournier, *The Meaning of Persons* (quoted in Keith Miller, *Habitation of Dragons* [Old Tappan, N.J.: Fleming H. Revell, 1993]).

23. William McNamara, *The Art of Being Human* (quoted in Keith Miller).

24. H.L. Mencken, quoted in Jon Winokur, ed., *The Portable Curmudgeon* (New York: Plume-Penguin, 1995).